Dora & Diego
Let's Cook

WILEY

John Wiley & Sons, Inc.

Published by John Wiley & Sons, Inc., Hoboken, New Jersey
Published simultaneously in Canada

Library of Congress Cataloging-in-Publication Data is available
upon request.

ISBN: 978-0470-63942-9

Printed in China

10 9 8 7 6 5 4 3 2 1

Senior Editor: Raina Moore

Designer: Michael Dawson

Nutritional Consultant: Lisa Sasson, Registered
Dietician and Clinical Associate Professor, NYU

Senior Content Manager: Brian Bromberg

Special thank you to: Cyma Zarghami, Marva Smalls,
Russell Hicks, Leigh Anne Brodksy, Dan Martinsen,
Paula Allen, Joanie Molina, and Madeira Ginley

John Wiley & Sons, Inc.

Publisher: Natalie Chapman

Associate Publisher: Jessica Goodman

Executive Editor: Anne Ficklen

Editor: Adam Kowit

Editorial Assistant: Cecily McAndrews

Production Director: Diana Cisek

Production Editor: Abby Saul

Manufacturing Manager: Kevin Watt

Waterbury Publications, Inc.

Contributing Editor and Writer: Lisa Kingsley

Design Director: Ken Carlson

Associate Design Director: Doug Samuelson

Production Assistant: Mindy Samuelson

Photography: Greg Scheidemann, Chris Hennessey

Recipe Developer and Food Stylist:
Charles Worthington

Food Stylist: Jennifer Peterson

Copy Editors: M. Peg Smith, Terri Fredrickson

CONTENTS

A Letter from the President

Dear Parents,

Welcome to Dora and Diego's world of great food, where the kitchen is an adventure, and healthy eating and nutrition are opportunities to discover new foods and flavors as you and your little ones explore—and play—together. Teach kids about good food when they are young and you have created a tradition of nutritious and delicious food choices that will have lifelong rewards.

As a mother of three young boys, I know how hard it can be to make food nutritional and fun. I love food, and I especially love sharing this passion with my kids. I hope this book helps you share your passion for preparing meals for your child and with your child. This is a kid-friendly cookbook the whole family can enjoy!

Modeling good eating habits is so important for kids—and Dora and Diego make it entertaining and achievable. Grabbing a glass of water when you're thirsty or a piece of fruit when you're hungry helps set the stage, as does talking with your kids about what makes them grow and how to fuel their bodies to play. It's a snap to bring these ideas to life with the recipes found here. At Nickelodeon, we want kids to understand how to create balance in their lives and how to make the right choices for themselves. A great introduction to food can only help them along the way and make family time more fun. For more than 10 years, Dora and Diego have been exploring and teaching kids, and now with this book, they will take your family on a wholesome cooking adventure.

Cyma Zarghami
President, Nickelodeon

Before You Get Started

Just like on an adventure, safety is most important when cooking with young children (see pages 10–11), but there are other things to remember too.

Patience is key. Young children accomplish tasks at different skill levels than adults—so the meatballs may be a little irregularly shaped. That's fine—it's all part of the adventure.

Things tend to get messy too. There will be flour on the floor, peanut butter smeared on the counter, and you both may need a change of clothes before dinner—and that's perfectly OK! When you sit down to eat the food you made together, the pride your child feels at having helped with such an important job will be apparent. Then you can both shout: "We did it! *¡Lo hicimos!*"

Cook and Learn

Cooking opens up a world of learning to a child. Here are just some of the life lessons to be learned in the kitchen.

GOOD NUTRITION When children help prepare a meal, they are more likely to try new foods.

FOLLOWING DIRECTIONS Children learn what a recipe is and that if they complete all of the steps in the right order, they will get the result they want—something yummy to eat!

SIMPLE MATH CONCEPTS Children can learn what's bigger—a cup or a half-cup—and how many half-cups equal a whole cup. Or they can count how many muffins a recipe makes.

SIMPLE SCIENCE CONCEPTS What happens when you put a liquid in the freezer? Or when you put water over heat? The simple processes used in the most basic cooking can teach your child about different states of matter.

VOCABULARY To a 3-year old, the language of cooking is all new. Kids can learn new words in English . . . *y en español!*

COMPARISON AND CONTRAST Little explorers can learn the difference between hot and cold, hard and soft, liquid and solid, raw and cooked, and fast and slow.

CAUSE AND EFFECT What happens when you stir the liquid ingredients into the dry ingredients? Why do muffins puff up when they bake? Children are naturally curious and love to discover new things!

COOPERATION Working together for a common good (such as fresh-baked cookies!) is a valuable life skill.

SELF-HELP SKILLS Accomplishing a kitchen task builds a sense of confidence that children can help take care of themselves.

READING SKILLS Looking at recipes with a parent helps children learn to recognize words and symbols.

CULTURAL AWARENESS Everyone cooks and eats, but each culture has special foods. Children can learn to appreciate differences while exploring the world of cooking and eating foods from other cultures.

How to Use this Book

The recipes in this book are created to appeal to young children—and to the rest of the family too. They call for real ingredients combined in a captivating way that encourages children to branch out and explore new things.

Children love to be involved in cooking. The Kids Help! symbol on selected steps of each recipe highlights a task that most children between the ages of 2 and 5 can easily accomplish. That task appears in a different color than the rest of the step. There is at least one Kids Help! task in every recipe. It might be as simple as stirring or as challenging as filling and rolling up a burrito. (See the opposite page for general guidelines on cooking with children and the age-appropriate jobs they can do.)

A note on yields: The number of servings represents a satisfying yet reasonable adult portion. Your child will likely not eat a whole serving, and leftovers are good to have!

Ready, Set, Cook!

Make meal planning an adventure. Sit down with your child and read through this book. Select a recipe or recipes that sound good. Help your child learn how to create a balanced meal—and make a game of it. (See "Menus with Map!" on page 122.) Make a grocery list, if necessary, to take to the store to go shopping. When you are ready to start cooking, read through the entire recipe, step-by-step, with your child. Stress the importance of washing hands before you begin cooking. Measure out ingredients ahead of time so the process goes as smoothly as possible and so you can take time to ask questions and talk about what you are doing.

Age-Appropriate Tasks

Most 5-year olds will have more advanced kitchen skills than most 2-year olds, but even children of the same age differ in maturity.

The recommendations below are adapted from guidelines for cooking with young children from the National Network for Child Care. Use them only as a starting point—you know your own child best.

The average 2-year old can

- scrub fruits and vegetables
- wipe the countertops and table
- dip one ingredient into another
- tear lettuce and spinach leaves into bite-size pieces
- crush crackers or corn chips into crumbs for breading
- sprinkle cheese
- snap fresh green beans
- arrange foods on a baking pan

The average 3-year old can do all of the above, plus

- pour measured liquids into a bowl of dry ingredients
- mix batter
- stir or whisk ingredients together
- shake a jar of homemade salad dressing
- spread peanut butter on firm bread
- cut soft foods, such as bananas, with a plastic serrated knife

The average 4- and 5-year old can do all of the above, plus

- mash soft foods
- measure dry and liquid ingredients
- peel a banana or an orange if skin has been loosened
- crack an egg into a bowl
- cut bread or cookie dough with cookie cutters
- shape meatballs
- set the table
- clear the table

¡Vamos a cocinar!
Let's cook!

Nutrition Notes

Because toddlers and preschoolers grow in spurts, their appetites come and go in spurts. They might eat everything in sight one day and almost nothing the next. That's perfectly normal—you just want to offer the right stuff when they're in an eating mood.

One of the most important nutrients for children this age is calcium, which is necessary to grow strong bones and teeth. And what drink is a great source of calcium? *¡La leche!* Milk—a drink most children love—is the best source of calcium. Soy or rice milk can be substituted for cow's milk.

The American Academy of Pediatrics recommends low-fat (1%) milk and yogurt, and part-skim cheeses for children over the age of 2. The recipes in this book call for low-fat milk.

Fiber is another important dietary component for young children. You can get a lot of fiber from *las frutas y los vegetales.* Fruits and vegetables are great sources of fiber, as are whole grains. That's why the recipes in this book call for brown rice—which has more fiber than white rice—and white whole wheat flour, which looks and acts like white flour but retains more fiber and nutrients than all-purpose bleached flour.

The following daily dietary recommendations come from the United States Department of Agriculture (USDA) and the American Academy of Pediatrics.

Age	Fruits	Vegetables	Grains	Meats & Beans	Milk	Oils
2-3	1 cup	1 to 1½ cups	3 ounces	2 ounces	2 cups	3 tsp.
4-5	1 to 1½ cups	1½ cups	4 to 5 ounces	3 to 4 ounces	2 cups	4 tsp.

Let's Move!
¡Vamos a mover!

Eating good-for-you food is just one piece of living a healthy life. Being physically active is also very important. Both Dora and Diego encourage kids to be active on their adventures because physical activity builds muscle and helps maintain a healthy body weight. It also helps children learn good habits early in life and gives them an outlet for their natural energy.

Try these playful and imaginative activities with your child.

TREE FROG HOP: Outdoors or in a large open room, invite your child to jump from spot to spot like a tree frog. Have him or her start with small jumps and build to jumps as high as possible. *¡Brinca!* Hop!

PASO PEQUEÑO/GRANDE PASO (LITTLE STEP/BIG STEP): Move around the room or yard with your child, sometimes taking tiny steps and sometimes giant steps. Let your child do it on his or her own, giving a signal (like two hand claps) that means it's time to switch from one kind of step to the other.

PINTO THE PONY GALLOP: Show your child how to gallop (lead with one foot while the other catches up). Make a game of Follow the Leader, galloping around the yard. Galloping for an extended period of time helps build a strong heart and lungs.

JUMP THE RIVER: Lay a jump rope in a straight line on the floor—or draw a line on the ground with chalk. Ask your child to pretend the line is a river and to jump from one side of the river to the other. When your child is ready, widen the river by using two ropes or lines side by side.

SWIPER'S HIDE-AND-SEEK: Choose an object that Swiper has "swiped"—such as a stuffed animal or ball—and hide it somewhere in your yard or in the park or playground. Ask your child to find what Swiper has swiped. As he or she gets closer to the object, give a signal (such as saying, "*¡Sí! Sí!*").

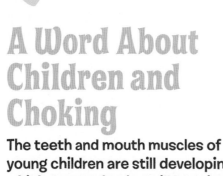

A Word About Children and Choking

The teeth and mouth muscles of young children are still developing, which means they're still learning how to chew and swallow properly. Prevent choking by avoiding certain foods or cutting them into pieces that are no larger than ½ inch.

The USDA lists the following as high-risk foods:

- Peanuts
- Chewing gum
- Popcorn
- Chips
- Tough meat
- Hard candy
- Round slices of hot dogs
- Carrot sticks or baby carrots
- Whole grapes
- Whole cherry or grape tomatoes
- Large pieces of raw fruits and vegetables
- Large cubes of cheese

To prevent choking:

- Cut food for your child into pieces no larger than ½ inch and teach him or her to chew food completely.
- Keep a close eye on your child while he or she is eating.

- Have your child eat at the table or at least while sitting down. Never allow your child to run, walk, play, or lie down with food in his or her mouth.
- Slice hot dogs and sausages lengthwise, then into half-moon slices.
- Cut grapes, cherry tomatoes, grape tomatoes, and other round foods in half.
- Cook carrots and celery sticks until slightly soft, grate them, or cut them into small pieces or thin matchsticks.
- Spread peanut butter thinly on bread or crackers. A thick glob of peanut butter can cause choking.

A Word About Food Allergies

It is estimated that 2% to 8% of toddlers and preschoolers have food allergies. As your child's culinary repertoire expands, he or she may be trying new foods, some of which are more likely to cause allergic reactions than others. These include peanuts, tree nuts such as walnuts and pecans, fish, shellfish, eggs, milk, soy, and wheat.

Use caution when feeding these foods to your child for the first time, and be sure if you're cooking with friends that you are aware of any allergies they may have.

Click's Kitchen Safety Snapshots

Click the Camera can show explorers how to stay safe on their kitchen adventure. Read Click's safety tips out loud with your child before you start cooking.

1. It is very important to always have a grown-up supervising you while you help in the kitchen. If you need help with a cooking job or you can't reach something you need, be sure to ask the grown-up to help you. Don't ever try to climb on a chair or counter to reach something.

2. Kitchen explorers get their own special spot to work. Your special spot should be far away from hot things, such as the stove and pots and pans. It should also be far away from sharp things, such as knives and scissors.

3. If your hair is long, tie it back. This keeps you from getting hair in the food you are making. It also keeps your hair from getting caught in cooking tools. If you have long sleeves, roll them up.

4. Before you touch food, wash your hands with soap and warm water. If you touch raw meat, wash your hands again. And don't put your fingers in your mouth after you touch food! If you have to sneeze or cough, do it into your hands and wash your hands before you go back to work.

5. The kitchen is full of sharp things, such as knives, food processor blades, blender blades, and scissors. Never touch any of these things. Let the grown-ups use the sharp stuff! Also, never touch the lid of a can that has been opened—it is very sharp!

6. Stay away from the hot stove unless you are with a grown-up. Grown-ups are also responsible for putting food in the oven, taking food out of the oven, and cooking food on top of the stove.

7. Remind the grown-up to be sure there are no pot handles sticking out from the stove and no knives or other sharp objects lying around.

¡Buenos DÍAS!

Good morning! It's time for a new day of adventure! But running with the animals all day takes a lot of energy! Eat a good breakfast, and you'll be ready to go, go, go like Diego!

Birds' Nests

ingredients

Nonstick cooking spray

5 cups frozen loose-pack shredded-style hash brown potatoes

5 eggs

2 tablespoons butter, melted

2 tablespoons canola oil

¼ teaspoon salt

⅓ cup shredded low-fat cheddar cheese

6 grape tomatoes, halved (optional)

RISE AND SHINE
SEE MENUS WITH MAP, PAGE 122

Let's make it! _¡Vámonos!_

1 Preheat oven to 425°F. Coat a large baking sheet with nonstick cooking spray. Place potatoes in a large bowl, breaking up any large clumps.

2 In a small bowl, beat 1 egg, butter, oil, and salt with a fork until well combined. Add egg mixture to potatoes and toss to coat completely. Divide potato mixture into 4 equal mounds 3 to 4 inches across. With the back of a spoon create a ¼-cup sized indention in center of each mound.

3 Bake in preheated oven for 25 minutes or until golden brown. Crack 1 of each of the remaining eggs into the mounds. Top with cheese. Bake for about 7 minutes until egg whites are set and yolk is almost cooked through, or to the doneness you'd like.

4 Transfer to plates and top with grape tomatoes, if you'd like.

Makes 4 servings.

Move with Boots! Celebrate making a great Bird's Nest by running and flapping your wings like a bird. Count how long you can do this!

15

Scrambled Eggs in River Rafts

ingredients

1 package refrigerated large whole wheat homestyle biscuits or homemade wheat rolls (see page 124)

4 eggs

¼ teaspoon salt

2 slices turkey bacon, cut into ¼-inch pieces

¼ cup chopped sweet red pepper

½ cup shredded low-fat Monterey Jack cheese

4 to 8 sweet red pepper strips, cut on an angle (optional)

Let's make it! ¡Vámonos!

1 Bake biscuits according to package directions. Leave oven on. When cool, cut out the top of 4 biscuits, leaving a ¼-inch border. With a fork, remove a portion of the biscuit center to create a bowl shape. Save the remaining biscuits for another use.

2 In a medium bowl, beat eggs and salt with a fork; set aside. Cook turkey bacon in a nonstick skillet on medium-high heat until beginning to brown; add chopped red pepper. Cook for 3 to 4 minutes until bacon is cooked and pepper is crisp-tender. **KIDS HELP!**

3 Add eggs to skillet. Cook without stirring until bottom begins to set. With a spatula, lift and fold cooked eggs so that uncooked portion flows underneath. Keep cooking and stirring for about 2 minutes or until eggs are cooked through.

4 Divide egg mixture among prepared biscuits. Top with cheese. Bake for 1 to 2 minutes or until heated through and cheese is melted. Transfer to plates. Arrange pepper strips to look like raft paddles, if you'd like. **KIDS HELP!**

Makes 4 servings.

¡Rápido!

Sweet red pepper strips are the paddles on these biscuit boats. That makes for one delicious river rafting adventure!

Tico's Nutty Stuffed French Toast

ingredients

- 2 eggs
- ½ cup low-fat milk
- 1 teaspoon vanilla extract
- ¼ teaspoon salt
- 6 ounces low-fat cream cheese
- 2 tablespoons granulated sugar
- ¼ cup chopped toasted pecans, walnuts, or almonds
- 8 slices firm-textured whole wheat bread
- 1 medium apple, peeled, cored, and thinly sliced
- 1 tablespoon butter
- Powdered sugar (optional)

Let's make it! *¡Vámonos!*

1 In a pie plate, whisk eggs, milk, vanilla, and salt.

2 In a small bowl, combine cream cheese, sugar, and nuts. Spread cheese mixture on 4 slices of bread. Arrange apple slices on cheese mixture. Top with remaining bread slices.

3 Place a stuffed piece of bread in egg mixture and soak for about 5 seconds. Carefully turn and soak other side for about 5 seconds. Transfer to a large plate. Repeat with remaining stuffed breads. Brush breads with any remaining egg mixture.

4 Melt butter in a large nonstick skillet. Cook stuffed toasts on medium heat for 4 to 5 minutes per side or until golden brown. Transfer to plates. Sift powdered sugar over toasts, if you'd like.

Makes 4 servings.

¡Perfecto!

19

Swiper's Blueberry Hill Muffins

ingredients

Nonstick cooking spray (optional)

- 1 cup white whole wheat flour
- ⅓ cup cornmeal
- ⅓ cup packed brown sugar
- 2 teaspoons baking powder
- ¼ teaspoon salt
- ⅔ cup low-fat plain yogurt
- ¼ cup canola oil
- 1 egg, beaten
- ¼ teaspoon vanilla extract
- 1 cup fresh or frozen blueberries

Let's make it! ¡Vámonos!

1 Preheat oven to 375°F. Line 24 mini muffin cups with paper liners. (Or spray cups with nonstick cooking spray.)

2 In a large bowl, combine flour, cornmeal, sugar, baking powder, and salt. In a medium bowl, combine yogurt, oil, egg, and vanilla. Add yogurt mixture to flour mixture. Stir until just combined. Add blueberries and fold in just until incorporated.

3 Divide batter among muffin cups and bake for about 15 minutes, until tops bounce back when touched lightly. Cool for 5 minutes before removing from pans.

Makes 24 mini muffins.

When Swiper isn't out trying to swipe, he lives on Blueberry Hill. No wonder he loves blueberries!

RISE AND SHINE

SEE MENUS WITH MAP, PAGE 122

20

Boots's Banana Pancakes

ingredients

- 2 ripe medium bananas
- 1 cup white whole wheat flour
- ¼ cup quick-cooking oats
- 1 tablespoon brown sugar
- 2 teaspoons baking powder
- ¼ teaspoon salt
- 1 cup low-fat milk
- 2 eggs, lightly beaten
- 1 tablespoon canola oil
- 1 banana, thinly sliced
- ½ cup maple syrup

Let's make it! ¡Vámonos!

1 Preheat oven to 250°F. In a medium bowl, mash 2 bananas with a fork until smooth.

2 In a large bowl, combine flour, oats, sugar, baking powder, and salt. In a medium bowl, combine milk, eggs, canola oil, and mashed banana. Stir banana mixture into flour mixture; batter will be slightly lumpy.

3 Heat a lightly greased griddle or a large heavy skillet on medium heat until a few drops of water dance across the surface. For each pancake, pour ¼ cup of batter onto griddle.

4 Cook until surface is bubbly and edges are slightly dry; turn and cook until pancakes are golden brown, about 1 to 2 minutes per side. Keep pancakes warm in oven in a loosely covered ovenproof dish while cooking remaining pancakes.

5 Meanwhile, in a small saucepan, heat sliced banana and maple syrup for 1 to 2 minutes until heated through and banana begins to soften. Serve maple-banana mixture over pancakes.

Makes 8 to 10 servings.

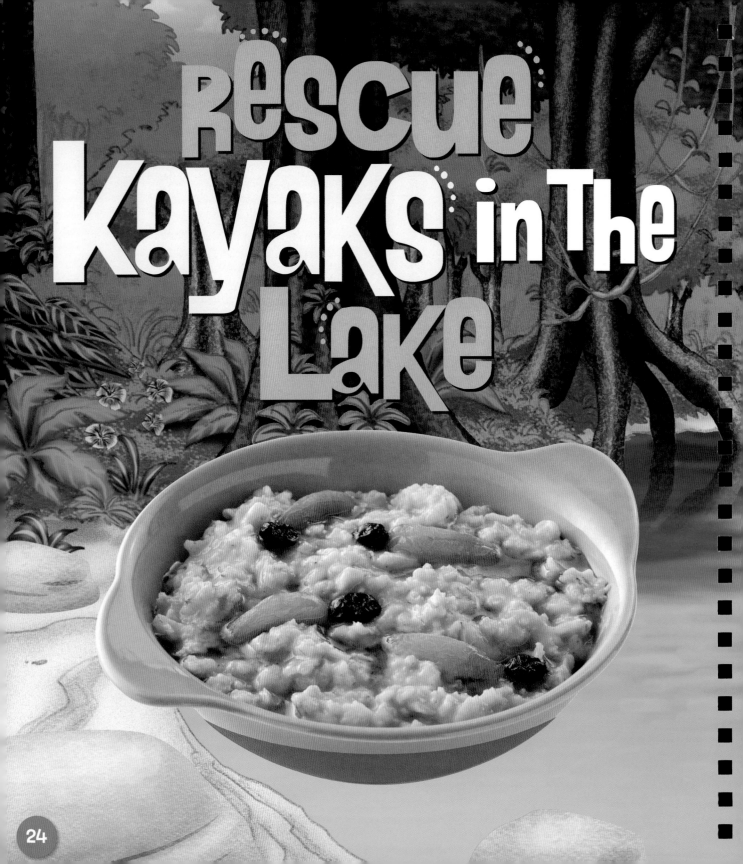

ingredients

- 4 cups water
- 1½ cups rolled oats
- Dash of salt (optional)
- ½ cup applesauce
- ¼ teaspoon cinnamon
- 1 6-ounce container low-fat vanilla yogurt
- ¼ cup maple syrup
- 4 dried apricots, cut into strips
- 2 tablespoons raisins or dried cranberries
- Additional maple syrup (optional)

The kayaks in this oatmeal are sweet pieces of dried fruit. *¡Las frutas!* How many different kinds of fruit can you name?

Let's make it! *¡A la cocina!*

1 In a medium saucepan, bring water to a boil. Stir in oats and, if using, salt. Reduce heat to medium; cook until oatmeal is tender, stirring often, about 6 minutes. Stir in applesauce and cinnamon and cook 1 minute.

2 Remove from heat; stir in yogurt and maple syrup. Divide oatmeal among 4 bowls. Arrange apricot strips and raisins to look like kayaks. Drizzle with additional maple syrup, if you'd like.

Makes 4 servings.

25

Benny's Breakfast Burritos

ingredients

- 6 eggs
- ½ teaspoon salt
- ¼ teaspoon ground black pepper
- 1 tablespoon butter
- ⅓ cup chopped tomatoes (optional)
- 4 6-inch whole wheat or multigrain tortillas, warmed
- ½ cup shredded low-fat cheddar cheese
- ½ cup mild salsa (optional)

Let's make it! *¡Vámonos!*

In a medium bowl, beat eggs, salt, and pepper with a whisk or fork.

In a 10-inch skillet, on medium-high heat melt butter. When butter begins to bubble, add egg mixture. Cook without stirring until bottom begins to set. With a spatula, lift and fold cooked eggs so that uncooked portion flows underneath. Stir in tomatoes, if you'd like. Continue cooking and stirring for about 2 minutes until eggs are cooked through.

Remove from heat and spoon one-fourth of egg mixture down center of each tortilla. Immediately sprinkle cheese over eggs; top with salsa, if you'd like. Fold in sides and roll up tortillas.

Makes 4 servings.

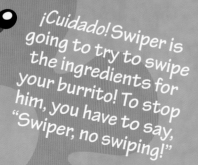

¡Cuidado! Swiper is going to try to swipe the ingredients for your burrito! To stop him, you have to say, "Swiper, no swiping!"

BUTTERFLY BREAKFAST QUESADILLAS

ingredients

4 7-inch whole wheat tortillas

1 tablespoon melted butter

6 ounces low-fat cream cheese,
   softened

2 tablespoons seedless
   strawberry preserves

1 ½ cups sliced strawberries

additional strawberries
(optional)

Let's make it! *¡Vámonos!*

1 Preheat oven to 400°F. Brush 1 side of each tortilla with melted butter. Arrange, buttered side down, on a large baking sheet.

2 In a small bowl, combine cream cheese and strawberry preserves. Divide and spread mixture on half of each tortilla. Top cheese mixture with 1½ cups sliced strawberries, and fold tortillas in half.

3 Bake for about 8 minutes, or until lightly brown. Cool for 1 to 2 minutes. Transfer to a cutting board and cut into wedges. Serve hot with additional strawberries, if you'd like.

Makes 4 servings.

In English, we say "butterfly." In Spanish, we say "*la mariposa.*" Put your quesadilla pieces in the shape of *la mariposa*.

FruiTy ForesT in a Cup

There are lots of ways to be an adventurer-like trying new foods. Be a fruit explorer! Are there any fruits you've never tried before?

ingredients

- 2 kiwifruits
- 1 cup blueberries
- 1 cup sliced strawberries
- 1 8-ounce can pineapple tidbits in pineapple juice
- 2 6-ounce containers strawberry-flavored low-fat yogurt
- 2 tablespoons chopped macadamia nuts

Let's make it! *¡Vámonos!*

1 Peel kiwis. Halve kiwis lengthwise. Lay flat side down and thinly slice. In four 8- to-10 ounce glasses or bowls, arrange kiwi, blueberries, and strawberries.

2 Drain pineapple tidbits, saving the juice. Pour pineapple juice over fruit in glasses. Divide the yogurt between fruit cups; top with pineapple and macadamia nuts.

Makes 4 servings.

Did you know that kiwifruit has even more vitamin C than oranges?

MiGhTy BITES and SupeR CooLeRs

All explorers and animal rescuers need to keep up their energy! To put some pep in your step, try these awesome snacks. And if you get thirsty on your adventure, keep cool with these drinks! Let's go!

Dora's Backpack Snack Pack

ingredients

- 1   cup round multigrain cereal
- ¾   cup mini pretzels
- 1½   tablespoons pepitas (pumpkin seeds)
- 1½   tablespoons slivered almonds
- 1   tablespoon peanut butter
- 2   teaspoons honey
- 1   teaspoon butter
-     Dash of chili powder
- ¼   cup chopped dried pineapple chunks

Let's make it! *¡Vámonos!*

1 Preheat oven to 375°F. In a medium bowl, combine cereal, pretzels, pepitas, and almonds.

2 In a small saucepan, combine peanut butter, honey, butter, and chili powder on medium heat. Cook and stir until mixture is warmed through and butter is melted. Pour over cereal mixture and stir gently to coat.

3 Spread mixture on a large baking sheet lined with parchment paper. Bake for 5 to 7 minutes until lightly toasted. Remove from oven and sprinkle with pineapple; stir to combine. When cool, store in an airtight container or transfer to small resealable plastic bags.

Makes 6 servings.

This tasty snack keeps well. Double or quadruple the recipe and package it in ½-cup servings to toss in a backpack for on-the-go snacks.

Yum, yum, yum, yum, yum! *¡Delicioso!*

DAY AT THE BEACH

SEE MENUS WITH MAP, PAGE 122

DiEGO'S SiLLy SnaKe STicKS

ingredients

Nonstick cooking spray

1 11-ounce package refrigerated breadsticks or homemade whole wheat dough (see page 124)

1 egg

1 tablespoon water

6 green or black olives, halved lengthwise

⅓ cup grated Parmesan cheese

Let's make it! *¡A la cocina!*

1 Preheat oven to 350°F. Spray 2 large baking sheets with nonstick cooking spray. Divide dough into 12 pieces. Unroll pieces and arrange on baking sheets. Stretch breadsticks to a length of about 15 inches and form into zigzags.

KIDS HELP!

2 In a small bowl, beat egg and water; brush on sticks. Press an olive half onto 1 end of the stick and sprinkle with cheese. Bake for 14 to 16 minutes until golden brown. Remove from baking sheet immediately; serve warm.

KIDS HELP!

Makes 12 servings.

Uh, oh! The Bobo Brothers are causing trouble! They'll mix up the ingredients! To stop them, say, "Freeze, Bobos!"

DIEGO'S RAINFOREST FIESTA

SEE MENUS WITH MAP, PAGE 122

ESTRELLITAS

ingredients

4 slices firm whole wheat bread

⅓ to ½ cup peanut butter

¼ cup raisins, dried cranberries, cherries, and/or snipped assorted dried fruits, such as papaya, mango, or apricots

¡Vamos a contar! How many points does a star have? ¡Uno, dos, tres, cuatro, cinco!

Let's make it! *¡Vámonos!*

1 Lightly toast bread. While still warm, cut out 1 star from each piece of bread with a 3- to 4- inch star cookie cutter.

KIDS HELP!

2 Spread peanut butter on star cutouts. Arrange dried fruits in peanut butter.

KIDS HELP!

Makes 4 servings.

TAPAS PARTY

SEE MENUS WITH MAP, PAGE 122

Dora's Empanadas

Let's make it! ¡Vámonos!

ingredients

- 1 15-ounce package refrigerated piecrust (2 crusts), softened according to package directions or homemade whole wheat crust (see page 124)
- Nonstick cooking spray
- ¾ cup salsa (optional)

1 Preheat oven to 400°F. On a lightly floured surface, roll crusts to 13-inch circles. Using a 3-inch cookie cutter, cut 24 rounds. Divide 1 of the fillings among the rounds, piling filling in center.

2 Lightly brush edges of rounds lightly with water. Fold rounds over to form crescents. Crimp edges with a fork to seal.

3 Spray a large baking pan with nonstick cooking spray. Transfer empanadas to baking pan and bake for 12 to 15 minutes until golden brown. Serve with salsa, if you'd like.

Makes 24 empanadas.

Cheesy Chicken Filling

In a medium bowl, combine:
- 1 cup finely chopped cooked chicken
- ¼ cup cooked peas
- ⅔ shredded low-fat cheddar cheese

Cheesy Broccoli Filling

In a medium bowl, combine:
- 1 cup finely chopped cooked broccoli
- ¼ cup finely shredded carrots
- ⅔ cup shredded low-fat cheddar cheese

After powering up on some empanadas, you can go exploring with a grown-up by taking a hike through your neighborhood.

TAPAS PARTY

SEE MENUS WITH MAP, PAGE 122

41

PiRaTe Pizza Coins

ingredients

Nonstick cooking spray

1   10-inch whole wheat or
     multigrain tortilla or wrap

½   cup pizza sauce

1   or more of the
     suggested toppers

½   cup grated low-fat
     mozzarella cheese

Let's make it! ¡Vámonos!

1 Preheat oven to 375°F. Spray a large baking pan with nonstick cooking spray. Using a 2- to 2½-inch cookie cutter, cut about 12 rounds out of the tortilla. Arrange rounds on baking pan.

2 With a small spoon, spread pizza sauce on tortilla rounds. Divide 1 or more toppings among rounds and top with cheese. Bake about 6 minutes or until cheese is bubbly.

Makes 4 servings.

Telescopes, like the one Pirate Boots has, help you see things far away.

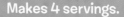

TAPAS PARTY

SEE MENUS WITH MAP, PAGE 122

toppers

- **1** cup chopped broccoli
- **1** cup chopped mushrooms
- **¾** cup chopped sweet red pepper
- **¾** cup drained pineapple tidbits
- **½** cup chopped olives
- **½** cup chopped cooked chicken
- **⅓** cup chopped sliced pepperoni
- **½** cup chopped ham

Ready to discover a yummy treasure? ¡Vámonos! Let's go!

Rainforest Rainbow Smoothie

ingredients

- 1 ½ cups chopped fresh or frozen mango
- 1 banana, cut up
- 1 6- to 8-ounce container low-fat vanilla yogurt
- 1 ½ cups ice
- ½ cup low-fat milk
- ½ cup sliced strawberries
- 4 whole strawberries (optional)

Let's make it! ¡A la aventura!

1 In a blender, combine mango, banana, yogurt, ice, and milk. Cover and blend until smooth. Divide about half of the mixture among 4 small glasses.

2 Add strawberries to blender; cover and blend until smooth. Gently pour strawberry mixture on top of mango mixture in glasses. Top with a whole strawberry, if you'd like.

Makes 4 servings.

KIDS HELP!

Sloths love to eat fruit from the trees where they "hang out!"

To make this smoothie extra-thick, use frozen bananas. Bananas that have been peeled and cut in large chunks last for weeks in the freezer in a tightly sealed container.

RISE AND SHINE

SEE MENUS WITH MAP, PAGE 122

Fizzy Fruit Punch

ingredients

- 2 cups orange juice
- 1 cup pineapple juice
- 1 cup chopped fresh pineapple
- 1 cup chopped fresh or frozen mango, or drained jarred mango
- 1 banana, chopped
- 1 tablespoon fresh lime juice
- chilled seltzer water or club soda
- lime, orange, or pineapple wedges (optional)

Let's make it! ¡Vámonos!

1 Combine orange juice, pineapple juice, pineapple, mango, banana, and lime juice in a 9x13-inch glass baking dish. Cover and freeze for 6 to 8 hours or until firm.

2 When ready to serve, remove from freezer. Let stand at room temperature for 10 to 15 minutes. With a spoon, scrape frozen fruit mixture to make a slush. Fill small glasses half-full with slush. Top with seltzer. Serve with a spoon and top with a fruit wedge, if you'd like.

Makes 6 servings.

This sweet, slushy, and bubbly drink is so refreshing when you've been outside on an adventure on a hot summer day!

TAPAS PARTY
SEE MENUS WITH MAP, PAGE 122

Alicia's Horchata

ingredients

- 2 cups uncooked long grain rice
- 3 cups warm water
- ⅓ cup sugar
- ½ teaspoon cinnamon
- 2 cups low-fat milk
- 1 cup cold water
- ice

FAMILY FIESTA

SEE MENUS WITH MAP, PAGE 122

Let's make it! *¡A la cocina!*

1 In a large bowl, combine rice and warm water. Cover and refrigerate overnight.

2 Transfer rice mixture to a blender. Cover and blend for 2 to 3 minutes, or until rice pieces are very small.

3 Strain liquid through several layers of cheesecloth into a pitcher. Add sugar and cinnamon. Add milk and 1 cup cold water. Taste it and add a little more sugar if you'd like. Cover and refrigerate until ready to serve. Stir before serving over ice.

Makes about 5 (8-ounce) servings.

Staying cool helps me to keep going on animal adventures!

Lemon-Lime Surprise

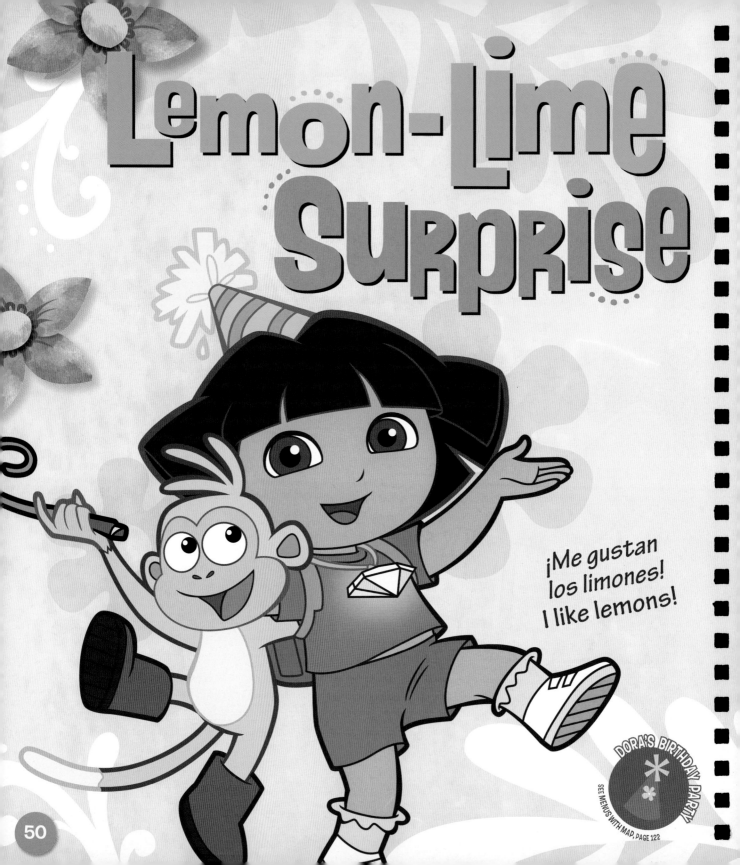

¡Me gustan
los limones!
I like lemons!

DORA'S BIRTHDAY PARTY
SEE MENUS WITH MAP, PAGE 122

ingredients

1 ½ cups water
1 cup sugar
3 ½ cups cold water
⅔ cup fresh lemon juice
⅔ cup fresh lime juice
ice
lemon and/or lime wedges
(optional)

Let's make it! *¡Vámonos!*

1 For lemon-limeade, in a medium saucepan over medium-high heat, combine 1 ½ cups water and sugar. Stir until sugar is completely dissolved. Transfer to a pitcher. Add cold water, lemon juice, and lime juice. Cover and refrigerate until ready to serve.

KIDS HELP!

2 Fill glasses with ice and top with lemon-limeade. Top with lemon and/or lime slices, if you'd like.

KIDS HELP!

Makes about 6 (8-ounce) servings.

Swiper is going to swipe a lemon! What do you need to say to stop him?

DINNER TIME ¡La Hora de Cena!

Going on adventures all day long can make any explorer hungry! These delicious dinner recipes will keep you strong and healthy and ready to keep exploring! *¡Vamos a cocinar!* Let's cook!

DieGo's MeaTball MöunTain RanGe

DIEGO'S RAINFOREST FIESTA
SEE MENUS WITH MAP, PAGE 122

ingredients

Nonstick cooking spray

- 1 egg, lightly beaten
- 3 tablespoons finely chopped onion
- 2 tablespoons dried bread crumbs
- 1 tablespoon grated Parmesan cheese
- ½ teaspoon dried Italian seasoning
- ½ teaspoon salt
- ½ cup cooked brown rice
- ¾ pound lean ground beef
- 2½ cups meatless pasta sauce
- 8 ounces dried whole wheat spaghetti
- 1 to 2 cups large cooked broccoli florets
- ¼ cup grated Parmesan cheese

This mountain range is *magnífico!* Eating the broccoli "trees" will help you grow big and strong so you can climb real mountains.

Let's make it! *¡A la aventura!*

1 Preheat oven to 350°F. Spray a 2½-quart rectangular or oval baking dish with nonstick cooking spray.

2 In a large bowl, combine egg, onion, bread crumbs, the 1 tablespoon cheese, Italian seasoning, and salt. Add rice and beef; mix well. On a piece of waxed paper, flatten meat mixture into a 1-inch-thick square. Cut the square into a grid to make 20 equal pieces.

3 Roll each piece into a meatball. Arrange in prepared dish and bake for about 15 minutes, or until internal temperature reaches 160°F. Meanwhile, in a large saucepan, heat pasta sauce over low heat. Transfer cooked meatballs to sauce and wipe out baking dish.

4 Cook spaghetti according to package directions; drain. Transfer spaghetti to baking dish. Add about ½ cup of sauce without meatballs; toss to coat. Arrange remaining sauce and meatballs on spaghetti in center of dish.

5 Arrange broccoli around edge to look like trees.

6 Loosely cover with foil and bake for 5 minutes. Top with remaining cheese and serve.
Note: Cut broccoli in small pieces before serving.

Makes 4 servings.

KIDS HELP!

Chicken Fingers with Mango-Pineapple Salsa

ingredients

- 1 8-ounce can crushed pineapple, undrained
- ½ cup chopped fresh mango or frozen mango, thawed
- 2 tablespoons finely chopped sweet red pepper (optional)
- 1 tablespoon chopped cilantro (optional)
- 1 tablespoon fresh lime juice
- 1 egg, lightly beaten
- ¼ cup light sour cream
- ½ teaspoon salt
- 1 pound boneless skinless chicken breast halves
- 4 cups tortilla chips

  Nonstick cooking spray

Let's make it! ¡Vámonos!

1 For the salsa, in a small bowl, combine pineapple, mango, sweet pepper (if you'd like), cilantro (if you'd like), and lime juice. Cover and refrigerate until ready to serve.

2 Preheat oven to 400°F. In a medium bowl, combine egg, sour cream, and salt. Cut chicken into ¾-inch thick strips and add to egg mixture. Stir to coat. Place chips in a 1-gallon resealable plastic bag. Use a rolling pin to crush to crumbs. Transfer to a pie plate or shallow dish. **KIDS HELP!**

3 Spray a large baking pan with nonstick cooking spray. Transfer a few chicken strips at a time to pie plate with crushed chips. Roll and press strips to coat all sides. Arrange on baking pan, leaving space between them. Bake for about 10 minutes, until chicken is no longer pink, turning after 5 minutes. Serve with salsa. **KIDS HELP!**

Makes 4 servings.

Tortilla chips can be white or yellow. In English, we say "white" and "yellow." In Spanish, we say "blanco" and "amarillo."

DORA'S BIRTHDAY PARTY
SEE MENUS WITH MAP, PAGE 122

Dora and Boots are dancing to tropical music! What dances do you like to do? Do one right now!

Mudslide Meatloaf and Gravy

ingredients

Nonstick cooking spray

¾	pound ground turkey
¾	pound lean ground beef
½	cup quick-cooking oats
½	cup chopped onion
½	cup finely chopped zucchini
1	egg, lightly beaten
¼	cup tomato sauce
1	tablespoon Dijon mustard
1	teaspoon dried oregano
1	tablespoon olive oil
1	tablespoon butter
8	ounces mushrooms, sliced
2	tablespoons flour
1	cup low-sodium chicken broth
½	cup low-fat milk
1	tablespoon low-sodium soy sauce

Let's make it! *¡A la cocina!*

1 Preheat oven to 375°F. Spray a 13x9-inch baking pan with nonstick cooking spray. Set aside. In a large bowl, combine turkey, beef, oats, onion, zucchini, egg, tomato sauce, mustard, and oregano. Mix until well combined.

2 In prepared pan, form the meat mixture into a loaf that measures about 5x10 inches. Bake for 40 to 50 minutes, or until internal temperature reaches 160°F.

3 Meanwhile, heat oil and butter in a medium skillet over medium-high heat until butter begins to bubble. Add mushrooms; cook for 4 to 5 minutes until mushrooms are just tender. Sprinkle flour over mushrooms and cook for 1 minute. Add broth, milk, and soy sauce to skillet. Bring to boil and cook for 2 minutes.

4 To serve, slice meatloaf and arrange on a platter. Pour Mudslide Gravy over slices.

Makes 6 servings.

Let's move! Go to the playground with a grown-up and imagine that the slide, swings, and see-saw are an Animal Rescuer Obstacle Course. How fast can you go through them all?

Fiesta Trio Frittata

ingredients

- 6 eggs
- 1 tablespoon water
- ¼ teaspoon salt
- ⅛ teaspoon pepper
- 1 stir-in choice
- 1 tablespoon olive oil
- ¼ cup shredded low-fat mozzarella

Let's make it! ¡Vámonos!

1 In a medium bowl, combine eggs, water, salt, and pepper. Use a fork or a whisk to mix really well. Add 1 stir-in and stir again to combine.

2 Heat oil in an 8-inch skillet over medium heat. Add egg mixture. As eggs begin to set, run a spatula around edge of skillet, lifting cooked eggs to allow uncooked portion to flow underneath. Continue until eggs are nearly set. Cover and cook for 2 minutes more.

3 Remove from heat; top with cheese. Return cover and let stand for 1 to 2 minutes until cheese softens. Cut into wedges and serve.

Makes 4 servings.

KIDS HELP!

FARMERS' MARKET FEAST

SEE MENUS WITH MAP, PAGE 122

Ham & Asparagus

1. cup cooked 2-inch pieces of asparagus
¾ cup chopped low-sodium ham, cubed
2. teaspoons snipped fresh dill or ½ teaspoon dried dill (optional)

Spinach & Tomato

⅔ cup wilted, well-drained, and chopped spinach (or thawed frozen spinach, well-drained)
⅓ cup chopped seeded tomato
2. tablespoons snipped fresh chives (optional)

Broccoli & Roasted Red Pepper

1. cup coarsely chopped cooked broccoli
⅓ cup chopped roasted red pepper
½ teaspoon dried Italian seasoning (optional)

Baked POTATO Rescue Boats

ingredients

- 2 large baking potatoes
- ¼ cup low-fat milk
- 1 3-ounce package low-fat cream cheese, softened
- ¼ teaspoon salt
- 1 topper
- ⅔ cup shredded low-fat cheddar cheese

Let's make it! ¡A la cocina!

1 Preheat oven to 400°F. Scrub potatoes and pierce in 2 to 3 places with a sharp knife. Bake in a shallow baking dish for 45 minutes to 1 hour until tender.

2 When potatoes are cool enough to handle, cut potatoes in half lengthwise. Carefully scoop flesh from potatoes into a medium bowl, leaving ¼ inch of potato on skin. Add milk, cream cheese and salt to bowl; mash until almost smooth. Return to potato skins. Arrange potatoes in baking dish.

3 Top potatoes with 1 of the toppers; lightly press into mashed potato. Top with cheese. Bake for 6 to 8 minutes until heated through and cheese is melted.

Makes 4 servings.

These stuffed baked-potato boats will rescue your family from hunger. ¡Al rescate!

Beef Taco Topper

In a small bowl, combine:

- 1 cup cooked lean ground beef
- ½ cup chunky salsa

Ham & Vegetable Topper

In a small bowl, combine:

- 1 cup cooked frozen mixed vegetables of choice
- ½ cup chopped low-sodium ham

Chicken & Broccoli Topper

In a small bowl, combine:

- 1 cup chopped cooked chicken
- ½ cup chopped cooked broccoli

Isa's Garden Pasta Salad

ingredients

- 6 ounces dried whole wheat penne pasta
- 1 cup snow peas, halved and strings removed
- 1 cup cubed cooked turkey
- 1 carrot, halved lengthwise and thinly sliced
- ⅓ cup diced sweet red pepper
- 1 green onion, sliced
- 2 tablespoons orange marmalade
- 1 tablespoon olive oil
- 1 tablespoon lime juice
- 1 teaspoon lime zest
- 1 teaspoon Dijon mustard
- ¼ teaspoon salt
- 1 11-ounce can mandarin oranges (juice pack), drained

Let's make it! ¡Vámonos!

1 Cook pasta according to package directions, adding snow peas for the last 2 minutes of cooking time. Rinse with cold water and drain. Transfer to a large bowl; add turkey, carrot, sweet pepper, and green onion.

2 In a small bowl, combine marmalade, olive oil, lime juice, lime zest, mustard, and salt; stir until well mixed. Pour over pasta mixture, toss to coat. Cover and refrigerate until ready to serve.

3 To serve, transfer to a serving platter. Top with mandarin oranges.

Makes 4 servings.

Lots of fruits and vegetables grow in a garden. How many fruits and vegetables do you count in your refrigerator?

FAMILY FIESTA

SEE MENUS WITH MAP, PAGE 122

64

Isa loves all the beautiful colors of her garden flowers. There are lots of beautiful colors in this pasta salad too. What *colores* do you see in this dish?

Jump Across The River Rocks

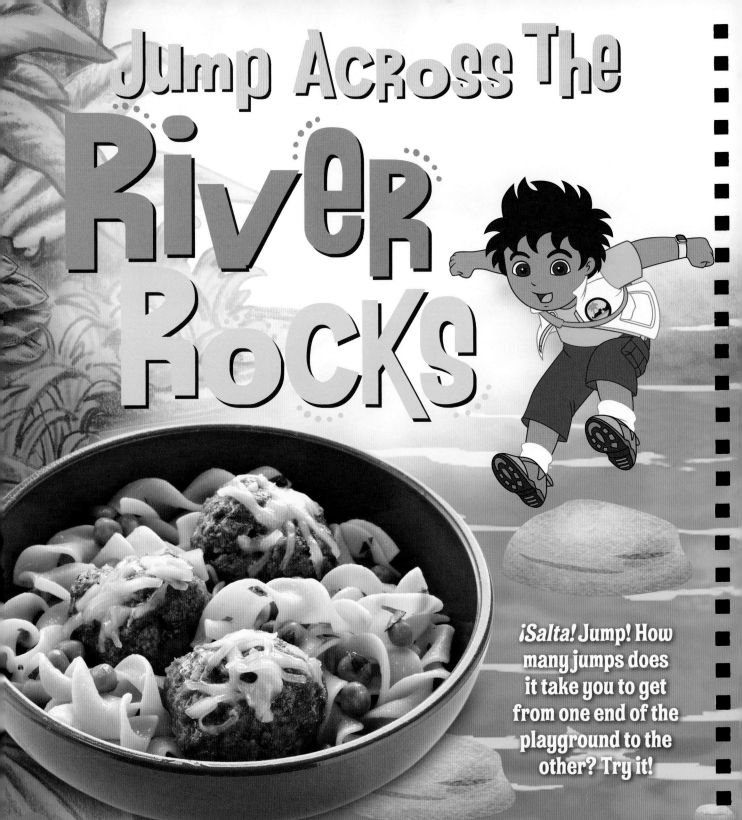

¡Salta! Jump! How many jumps does it take you to get from one end of the playground to the other? Try it!

ingredients

Nonstick cooking spray

¾ pound ground turkey

⅓ cup finely shredded carrot

¼ cup dried bread crumbs

1 egg white, lightly beaten

2 tablespoons snipped cilantro (optional)

½ teaspoon salt

¼ teaspoon mild chili powder (optional)

¼ teaspoon ground cumin

⅓ cup shredded low-fat Monterey Jack cheese

8 ounces egg noodles

1 cup frozen peas

2 tablespoons butter

snipped cilantro (optional)

Let's make it! *¡A la aventura!*

1 Preheat oven to 375°F. Spray a baking sheet with nonstick cooking spray. In a medium bowl, mix turkey, carrot, bread crumbs, egg white, cilantro (if you'd like), salt, chili powder (if you'd like), and cumin until well combined. On waxed paper, flatten mixture in a 1-inch-thick rectangle. Cut in a 15-portion grid to divide evenly. With moistened hands, form pieces into slightly flat meatballs. (Be sure to wash your hands when you're done.) Place meatballs on the baking sheet.

2 Bake for 20 to 25 minutes, or until browned and meatballs reach an internal temperature of 160°F. Top with cheese. Bake 1 to 2 minutes more or until cheese is melted.

3 Meanwhile, cook egg noodles according to package directions, adding peas for the last 3 to 4 minutes of cooking time. Cook until noodles and peas are tender. Drain and return to pan. Add butter and toss to coat. Divide noodles among 4 shallow bowls or plates and top with meatballs. Sprinkle with additional cilantro, if you'd like.

Makes 4 servings.

Chicken Taco Salad

ingredients

½ cup mild picante sauce or salsa

1½ cups coarsely chopped cooked chicken

5 cups shredded lettuce

1½ cups coarsely chopped cooked broccoli florets

⅓ cup shredded carrots

Taco toppers of your choice such as shredded cheddar cheese, sliced black olives, cilantro, chopped tomato, low-fat sour cream, and/or salsa

Music and taco salad make for una fiesta fantástica!

Let's make it! ¡Vámonos!

1 In a small skillet, over medium heat combine picante sauce and chicken. Cook for about 3 minutes just until heated through; set aside.

2 Divide lettuce among 4 plates. Top with broccoli, carrots, and chicken mixture. Serve with bowls of taco toppers.

Makes 4 servings.

KIDS HELP!

Swiper is going to try to swipe the fork! What do you say to stop Swiper from swiping el tenedor?

COOKING WITH ABUELA

SEE MENUS WITH MAP, PAGE 122

Fish in The Pond
TORTILLA SOUP

ingredients

- 2 teaspoons olive oil
- ¼ cup chopped onion
- 1 clove garlic, chopped
- 3 cups low-sodium chicken broth
- 1 14.5-ounce can Mexican-style diced tomatoes
- 1 cup frozen corn
- ½ teaspoon mild chili powder
- 1 cup chopped cooked chicken
- 1 small corn tortilla, cut into thin bite-size strips
- ⅓ cup fish-shape cheddar-flavored crackers

Let's count the fish in the pond! Uno, dos, tres, cuatro, cinco, seis, siete, ocho, nueve, diez.

Let's make it! ¡A la aventura!

1 In a large saucepan, cook onion and garlic in hot oil on medium-high heat for about 3 minutes or just until tender. Add broth, tomatoes, corn, and chili powder. Cook for 5 to 7 minutes or until corn is tender.

2 Add chicken and tortilla strips to soup and cook for 1 to 2 minutes until heated through. Ladle into 4 bowls. Top with fish crackers.

Makes 4 servings.

KIDS HELP!

COOKING WITH ABUELA

SEE MENUS WITH MAP, PAGE 122

Alphabet Forest Soup

ingredients

- 2   teaspoons canola oil
- ⅓   cup thinly sliced celery
- ¼   cup chopped onion
- ¼   teaspoon dried basil
- 2   cups favorite frozen vegetable blend
- ⅓   cup shredded carrots
- 3   cups low-sodium chicken broth
- ⅔   cup dried alphabet noodles
- 1½   cups chopped or shredded cooked chicken
- 1   cup baby spinach (optional)

Soup is great for warming up on a rainy day. How else do you keep warm and dry on rainy days?

Let's make it! ¡Vámonos!

1 In a large saucepan, cook celery, onion, and basil in hot oil on medium-high heat for 3 minutes. Add vegetable blend, carrots, and chicken broth; bring to a simmer. Add noodles and cook for 7 minutes or until vegetables and noodles are tender. If using spinach, tear the leaves in small pieces.

2 When ready to serve, add chicken and torn spinach, if you'd like. Cook for about 2 minutes until heated through.

Makes 4 servings.

Fish sTicks
wiTh Lime TarTar Sauce

ingredients

½ cup light mayonnaise

1 tablespoon lime juice

1 teaspoon lime zest

2 tablespoons finely chopped pickle or pickle relish

Nonstick cooking spray

1 egg, lightly beaten

1 pound cod filet, cut into ½-inch thick strips

1½ cups cheese-flavored snack crackers or panko bread crumbs

Let's make it! ¡A la cocina!

1 In a small bowl, combine mayonnaise, lime juice, and zest. Transfer half of mixture to a medium bowl. For Lime Tartar Sauce, add pickle to mixture remaining in small bowl; cover and refrigerate until ready to serve.

2 Preheat oven to 400°F. Spray a large baking pan with nonstick cooking spray. Add egg to remaining mayonnaise mixture in medium bowl; stir to combine. Add fish to bowl and toss gently to coat. Place crackers in a 1-gallon resealable bag. Use a rolling pin to crush into crumbs. Transfer to a pie plate or shallow dish.

3 Transfer a few fish strips at a time to pie plate. Roll and press strips to coat all sides. Arrange on baking pan, leaving space between them. Bake for about 10 minutes or until fish flakes when tested with a fork. Serve with Lime Tartar Sauce.

Makes 4 servings.

You can use either white cheddar or yellow cheddar crackers for the crispy breading on these fish sticks.

Shrimp and Veggie STir-FrY

This recipe calls for sweet red peppers, but you could use sweet yellow peppers instead–or even a mix of both.

ingredients

- 2 tablespoons rice wine vinegar
- 2 tablespoons low-sodium soy sauce
- 2 tablespoons apricot or peach preserves
- 1/3 cup water
- 1 teaspoon grated fresh ginger
- 2 teaspoons cornstarch
- 1 tablespoon canola oil
- 1 cup small broccoli florets
- 1 cup bite-size strips of sweet red pepper
- 1/2 cup thin matchstick-cut carrots or coarsely shredded carrots
- 1 pound medium shrimp, peeled and deveined (or 12 ounces precleaned shrimp)
- 2 green onions, thinly sliced
- 1/2 cup halved grape tomatoes
- 2 cups cooked brown rice

Let's make it! ¡Vámonos!

1 In a small bowl, combine vinegar, soy sauce, preserves, water, ginger, and cornstarch; set aside.

2 In a large skillet or wok, heat oil on medium-high heat. Add broccoli, sweet pepper, and carrots. Cook for 7 to 8 minutes or just until vegetables are crisp-tender. Remove from skillet with slotted spoon and keep warm.

3 Stir vinegar mixture and add to skillet. Cook and stir until bubbling and slightly thick. Add shrimp and onions to skillet and cook for about 3 minutes or until shrimp is opaque. Return vegetables to skillet, along with tomatoes. Heat through and serve with rice.

Makes 4 servings.

What color is broccoli?
¡Sí, es verde! Green!

Spectacular SIDES!

¡Al rescate! Make any main dish a spectacular success by pairing it with one of these slamming side dishes!

BackPack's
Salad Bundles

How many vegetables do you count packed into each lettuce wrap?

Yum, yum, yum, yum, yum! ¡Delicioso!

ingredients

- ⅓ cup low-fat sour cream
- ¼ cup salsa
- 2 romaine leaves
- ½ red sweet pepper, cut into thin strips
- 4 inches of a seedless cucumber, cut into thin strips
- 1 carrot, cut into thin strips
- ½ cup thin strips of jicama

Let's make it! *¡Vámonos!*

1 In a small bowl, combine sour cream and salsa. Divide among 4 small bowls.

2 Cut romaine leaves in half lengthwise and remove the center rib.

3 Lay one-fourth of the vegetable strips across the end of 1 lettuce leaf. Roll up and place on a plate, seam side down. Repeat with remaining vegetables. Serve each with a small bowl of dressing.

Note: To transport, store in an ice-packed cooler.

Makes 4 servings.

DAY AT THE BEACH

SEE MENUS WITH MAP, PAGE 122

SCARLET MACAW COLESLAW

Ingredients

- 1 8-ounce can pineapple tidbits, juice pack
- 3 cups purchased coleslaw mix
- 1 orange, peeled, pith removed, and cut into bite-size pieces
- ¼ cup diced sweet yellow pepper
- 1 green onion, thinly sliced (optional)
- ⅓ cup chopped fresh mango or frozen mango, thawed
- 1 tablespoon rice wine vinegar
- 1 tablespoon canola oil
- ¼ teaspoon salt

Let's make it! ¡A la cocina!

1 Drain pineapple, saving the juice. In a medium bowl, combine pineapple, slaw mix, orange, sweet pepper, and onion, if you'd like.

2 For the mango dressing, in a blender, combine mango, vinegar, oil, and salt; blend. Add pineapple juice, 1 tablespoon at a time, until mixture has a smooth consistency. Scrape with a spatula as necessary.

3 Pour mango dressing over coleslaw mixture; stir to combine. Cover and refrigerate until ready to serve—no more than 3 hours. Stir again before serving.

Makes 4 to 6 servings.

DORA'S BIRTHDAY PARTY

SEE MENUS WITH MAP, PAGE 122

Scarlet macaws love to eat fruits like mango, orange, and pineapple that are in this special slaw!

83

Surfing Safari Fruit Salad Stacks

ingredients

- 2 ¼-inch-thick fresh pineapple slices, peeled and cored
- 1 orange, peel and pith removed, sliced ¼ inch thick
- 2 kiwifruits, peeled, quartered, and sliced ¼ inch thick
- 1 banana, sliced ¼ inch thick
- ¼ cup green grapes, halved
- ¼ low-fat yogurt
- 1 tablespoon lime juice
- 1 tablespoon honey

Let's make it! *¡A la aventura!*

1 Cut pineapple and oranges into ½- to 1-inch pieces. On small plates, make stacks of fruit about 2 inches high.

2 In a small bowl, combine yogurt, lime juice, and honey. Drizzle dressing on stacks.

Makes 6 to 8 servings.

¿Alta or *corta?* Make your salad stacks as tall or short as you like. Either way, they are *excelente!*

DIEGO'S RAINFOREST FIESTA

SEE MENUS WITH MAP, PAGE 122

Silly Face Salad

ingredients

- ¼ cup orange juice
- 1 green onion, sliced (white portion only)
- 1 tablespoon fresh lemon juice
- 2 teaspoons Dijon mustard
- 2 tablespoons olive oil
- 2 carrots, peeled
- 2 cups shredded lettuce or whole lettuce leaves
- ½ cucumber, sliced
- ½ cup grape tomatoes, halved, or thin wedges of tomato
- ¼ cup green or black olives, halved
- Fresh herbs sprigs, such as dill, parsley, or basil

FARMERS' MARKET FEAST

SEE MENUS WITH MAP, PAGE 122

Let's make it! ¡Vámonos!

1 For dressing, in a blender, combine orange juice, green onion, lemon juice, and mustard. Blend until onion is minced. With blender running on low speed, slowly add olive oil. Transfer to a small container; set aside until ready to serve.

2 Cut carrots into small bite-size slices and/or use a peeler to create thin carrot ribbons. On 4 salad plates, place lettuce leaves and use carrots and other vegetables and herbs to make silly faces.

3 When ready to serve, drizzle with dressing.

Makes 4 servings.

The tomato lips on this silly salad are rojo. What other colors do you see?

KIDS HELP!

Hop-Along Glazed Carrots

ingredients

- 1 pound baby carrots
- 3 tablespoons packed brown sugar
- 1 tablespoon butter
- 1 tablespoon low-sodium soy sauce
- 1 teaspoon toasted sesame seeds

Let's make it! *¡A la cocina!*

1 In a medium saucepan, combine carrots and enough water to cover. On medium-high heat, bring to a boil and cook for 5 to 7 minutes just until tender. Drain completely and return to saucepan.

2 Add brown sugar, butter, and soy sauce. Cook and stir for 2 to 3 minutes or until carrots are glazed. Transfer to serving bowl. Sprinkle with sesame seeds.

Makes 4 to 6 servings.

KIDS HELP!

To toast sesame seeds, spread in a small skillet placed over medium heat and stir often so they don't burn.

BRoCColi ConQueso

There's that Swiper again. He's going to swipe *el queso*. What do you say to stop him from swiping?

ingredients

- ½ cup low-fat milk
- 1 tablespoon flour
- ¼ teaspoon salt
- ⅓ cup shredded low-fat cheddar cheese
- 3 cups broccoli florets

Let's make it! ¡Vámonos!

1 For the cheese sauce, in a small jar, combine milk, flour, and salt; cover and shake until completely blended. In a small saucepan on medium heat, cook milk mixture, stirring continuously, until milk begins to steam. Continue cooking for 2 to 3 minutes until mixture is thickened and begins to bubble.

2 Remove from heat and stir in cheese until melted. Cover and keep warm.

3 Meanwhile, steam broccoli in stovetop steamer over boiling water for 3 to 5 minutes until it's done how you like it. Cut broccoli in small pieces. Transfer to a serving bowl and spoon cheese sauce over.

Makes 6 servings.

Benny the Bull has a big appetite! He loves to eat vegetables. How many vegetables can you name? How many do you see in your kitchen?

Misión Cumplida Mash

ingredients

3 medium Yukon gold or other starchy potatoes (about ¾ pound), peeled and quartered

2 carrots, peeled and cut into 2-inch pieces

¼ cup low-fat milk

1 tablespoon butter

¼ teaspoon salt

¼ teaspoon pepper

Let's make it! *¡A la aventura!*

1 In a medium saucepan, combine potatoes, carrots, and enough water to cover. On medium-high heat, bring to a boil and cook for about 10 minutes until potatoes and carrots are tender.

2 Drain vegetables and return to pan. Add milk, butter, salt, and pepper. Mash with a potato masher until it's a consistency you like. **Transfer to a serving bowl.**

Makes 4 servings.

KIDS HELP!

Spanish Rice

ingredients

- 1 tablespoon olive oil
- ¼ cup chopped onion
- ¼ cup chopped celery
- ¼ cup chopped carrot
- 1 clove garlic, minced
- ½ teaspoon cumin (optional)
- ¼ teaspoon salt
- ½ cup frozen peas
- 1 6-ounce can tomato sauce
- 4 cups cooked brown rice (two 8.8-ounce packages ready rice)
- 3 tablespoons snipped cilantro (optional)

Let's make it! ¡Vámonos!

1. In a large skillet on medium-high heat, cook onion, celery, carrot, garlic, cumin (if you'd like), and salt in hot oil for about 4 minutes just until vegetables are tender. Add peas and tomato sauce and cook for 5 minutes or until peas are tender.

2. Add rice to skillet; cook and stir for 3 to 4 minutes until heated through. Transfer to a serving bowl. Sprinkle with cilantro, if you'd like.

Makes 6 to 8 servings.

KIDS HELP!

Boots calls this rice,
and Tico calls it *arroz*.
Say it both ways!
Whatever you call it,
we're sure you'll call
it *delicioso!*

Delicious DESSERTS

¡Postres Perfectos!

Special days call for special treats! Cakes and cookies are perfect for parties. *¡A la fiesta!*

CRYSTAL KINGDOM JEWEL CUPS

ingredients

1 ¼ cups boiling water

1 package (8 servings) fruit-flavor gelatin

3 cups blueberries, raspberries, and/or sliced strawberries

½ cup low-fat whipped topping

Let's make it! ¡Vámonos!

1 In a medium bowl, combine boiling water and gelatin. Stir for about 2 minutes or until gelatin is completely dissolved. Pour into an 8x8-inch pan. Refrigerate for 2 to 3 hours or until firm.

2 Dip bottom of pan in warm water for 10 seconds. Using very small cookie cutters, cut gelatin into bite-size shapes. (Or use a knife to cut into bite-size diamonds and squares).

3 To serve, divide fruit and gelatin among 8 bowls. Top with whipped topping.

Makes 8 servings.

Quick! You need to stop Swiper from swiping the fruit! What do you need to say?

¿Qué colores? What colors do you see in the bowl? What fruits do you see?

Bobo Brothers' Banana Bowls

ingredients

- 2 cups vanilla, strawberry, or chocolate ice cream
- 1 banana, sliced
- 1 8-ounce can crushed pineapple, drained
- ¼ cup chocolate fudge ice cream topping, warmed
- ½ cup low-fat whipped topping
- 2 small strawberries, halved (optional)

Let's make it! ¡A la aventura!

1 Divide ice cream among 4 bowls. Top with banana and pineapple.

2 Drizzle with chocolate ice cream topping.

3 Top each with whipped topping and a strawberry half, if you'd like.

Makes 4 servings.

Let's *move!* Pretend you're a monkey. How do monkeys move? Swing from a swing and pretend it's a vine–or play on the monkey bars!

The Bobo Brothers don't mean to make mischief. They just can't help monkeying around!

ingredients

- 32 reduced-fat vanilla wafer cookies
- 1 ½ cups vanilla and/or chocolate ice cream, softened slightly
- ⅓ cup low-fat chocolate fudge ice cream topping, warmed
- 2 tablespoons finely chopped macadamia nuts (optional)

These are great to have in the freezer when *amigos* come over and need to cool down from a hot day of adventure!

Let's make it! *¡A la cocina!*

1 On a baking sheet lined with parchment paper, arrange 16 wafers, flat side up. Using a small cookie dough scoop or spoon, top each wafer with about 1 ½ tablespoons of the ice cream.

2 Top ice cream with remaining wafers, flat side down. Press lightly to flatten ice cream. Freeze for 20 minutes.

3 Using a small spoon, divide fudge topping among cookie sandwiches, spooning over tops. Sprinkle with nuts immediately, if you'd like. Cover and freeze for 1 to 2 hours or until firm.

Makes 16 sandwiches.

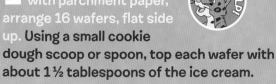

Abuela's OaTmeaL BiTes

ingredients

1½ cups rolled oats, quick or old-fashioned

1 cup white whole wheat flour

¼ cup packed brown sugar

¼ cup wheat germ

½ teaspoon baking powder

¼ teaspoon baking soda

½ teaspoon salt

⅓ cup canola oil

½ cup applesauce

1 egg, lightly beaten

½ cup raisins or golden raisins (optional)

Let's make it! ¡Vámonos!

1 Preheat oven to 375°F. In a large bowl, combine oats, flour, sugar, wheat germ, baking powder, baking soda, and salt; stir to mix thoroughly. In a medium bowl, combine oil, applesauce, and egg.

2 Add applesauce mixture to oats mixture; add raisins, if you'd like. Mix with a wooden spoon until blended. **KIDS HELP!**

3 Drop by rounded tablespoons on ungreased baking sheets 2 inches apart. Bake for 8 to 10 minutes until bottoms are lightly brown. Cool on pan for 1 to 2 minutes; transfer to rack. **KIDS HELP!**

Makes about 24 cookies.

You can use raisins—or any kind of dried fruit you like—in these chewy cookies. Try dried cranberries or cherries, or snipped dried apricots.

COOKING WITH ABUELA

SEE MENUS WITH MAP, PAGE 122

Rainforest Fruit Pops

Let's make it! ¡A la aventura!

1 In a small saucepan, sprinkle gelatin over nectar. Let stand for 4 minutes. Cook and stir on medium heat until gelatin is dissolved. Remove from stove.

2 In a blender, combine yogurt, fruit, and nectar mixture. Cover and blend until smooth. Divide mixture among eight 3- to 5-ounce paper cups. Cover cups with small squares of foil. Cut a small slit in the center of each piece of foil. Insert a food-safe crafts stick. Freeze for 4 hours or until firm.

3 To serve, remove foil and tear paper cup away.

Makes 8 servings.

ingredients

- 1 teaspoon unflavored gelatin
- ½ cup mango, papaya, or apricot nectar
- 2 6-ounce containers low-fat vanilla yogurt
- 1 cup chopped mango or stawberries

If you have a mold for making frozen treats, you can use it instead of the paper cups, foil, and crafts sticks.

Incan Quinoa Pudding

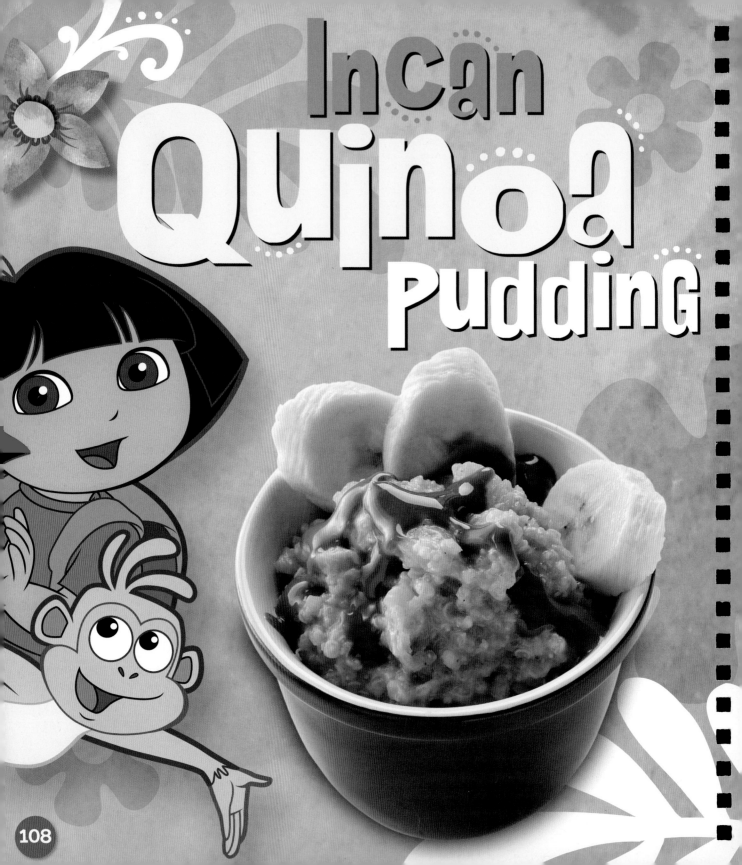

ingredients

- 3 cups apple juice
- 1 cup quinoa
- ½ cup chopped dried apricots
- 1 cup low-fat milk, plus 2 to 3 tablespoons
- 2 eggs
- ¼ cup honey
- ¼ teaspoon cinnamon
- 2 small bananas, sliced
- ¼ cup dulce de leche or caramel ice cream topping, warmed

¡Dulce! Sweet! Dulce de leche is a sweet caramel-flavored sauce that is delicious on pudding and ice cream!

Let's make it! *¡Vámonos!*

1 In a large saucepan on medium-high heat, bring apple juice, quinoa, and apricots to a boil. Reduce heat to medium-low and simmer, stirring occasionally, for 15 to 20 minutes or until quinoa is tender.

2 Meanwhile, in a medium bowl, whisk the 1 cup milk, eggs, honey, and cinnamon until well blended. While stirring, slowly add egg mixture to cooked quinoa. Cook, stirring constantly, for 3 to 5 minutes or until thickened. (Pudding will coat the back of a spoon.)

KIDS HELP!

3 Transfer pudding to medium bowl; cool slightly. Cover surface with plastic wrap and refrigerate for 2 to 3 hours until fully chilled.

4 To serve, spoon into dessert bowls. Top with banana slices. Thin dulce de leche with 2 to 3 tablespoons of milk, if necessary. Drizzle pudding with dulce de leche.

KIDS HELP!

Makes 8 servings.

Monkey Business Monkey Bread

Is this bread big or little?
¿Grande o pequeño?
Answer in English . . .
y en español!

ingredients

- 2 (1-pound) loaves frozen whole wheat bread dough, thawed according to package directions
- 1 cup packed brown sugar
- ½ cup granulated sugar
- 1 teaspoon cinnamon
- 1 medium apple, peeled, cored, and chopped (about 1⅔ cup)
- ½ cup raisins
- 2 tablespoons orange juice
- ¼ cup butter
- ⅓ cup orange juice
- Nonstick cooking spray

Let's make it! *¡Vámonos!*

1 Cut each loaf into 24 pieces. In a medium bowl, combine brown sugar, granulated sugar, and cinnamon. In another medium bowl, combine apple, raisins, and 2 tablespoons juice; toss to coat.

2 Place butter and ⅓ cup orange juice in a small microwave-safe bowl and heat in microwave oven for 1 minute; stir and keep heating for 10 to 15 seconds at a time until butter is melted. Heavily coat a 10-inch fluted tube pan with nonstick cooking spray.

3 Dip bread pieces in butter mixture; shake off extra butter. Transfer to sugar mixture; roll to coat. Arrange in prepared pan, layering with apples and raisins. Top with any remaining butter, sugar, and apple mixtures.

4 Cover and let rise in a warm place for 35 to 45 minutes until doubled. Uncover and bake in a preheated 350°F oven for about 35 minutes until bread is golden brown and sounds hollow when tapped. Cover loosely with foil the last 10 minutes of baking to prevent overbrowning. Remove from oven and let cool 2 minutes. Turn over onto a serving platter and remove pan. Let cool 10 minutes.

Makes 16 servings.

Diego's Dessert Crisps
with Mango Custard Cream

ingredients

- 1½ cups chopped fresh or frozen (thawed) mango
- 4 ounces low-fat cream cheese, softened
- ¼ cup dulce de leche or caramel ice cream topping
- ¼ cup mango nectar
- 1 8-ounce container low-fat frozen whipped topping, thawed
- 2 tablespoons granulated sugar
- ½ teaspoon cinnamon
- 2 5- to-6-inch whole wheat or multigrain tortillas
- 1 tablespoon butter, melted

If you'd like, substitute peaches or strawberries for the mango in the custard cream.

Let's make it! ¡A la aventura!

1 For Mango Custard Cream, combine mango, cream cheese, dulce de leche, and mango nectar in a blender. Blend until completely smooth, scraping with a spatula as needed. (Add more nectar, 1 tablespoon at a time, if necessary). Transfer to a large bowl.

2 Fold about one-third of whipped topping into mango mixture until well combined. Fold remaining whipped topping until just combined; cover and refrigerate for 2 to 3 hours until set.

3 For Dessert Crisps, preheat oven to 375°F. In a small bowl, combine sugar and cinnamon. Brush tortillas with butter and sprinkle with sugar mixture. With a pizza cutter or knife cut tortillas into ½- to 1-inch-wide strips.

4 Transfer to a large baking sheet, sugar side up, and bake for 5 to 7 minutes or until crisp. Transfer to a plate and let cool. Serve with Mango Custard Cream.

Makes 6 to 8 servings.

FARMERS' MARKET FEAST

SEE MENUS WITH MAP, PAGE 122

Boots's Choco Banana Cake

ingredients

- ¾ cup butter (1 ½ sticks), room temperature
- 1 cup granulated sugar
- 2 eggs
- 1 cup mashed ripe banana
- 1 ¾ cups unbleached all-purpose flour
- ¼ teaspoon salt
- ¾ teaspoon baking soda
- ⅓ cup buttermilk
- 1 teaspoon vanilla extract
- ½ cup dulce de leche
- 2 bananas, sliced
- 1 cup semisweet chocolate pieces
- ½ cup heavy cream
- ¼ cup chopped macadamia nuts (optional)

Let's make it! ¡Vámonos!

1 Preheat oven to 350°F. Grease and flour two 9-inch round cake pans.

2 In a large mixing bowl, beat butter and sugar on medium until well combined. Add eggs, 1 at a time, beating well after each addition. Add banana and stir until combined. In a medium bowl, combine flour, salt, and baking soda; mix well. Add to egg mixture and stir until combined. Add buttermilk and vanilla; stir until combined.

3 Pour into prepared pans. Bake for 20 to 25 minutes or until a toothpick inserted into center of cakes comes out clean. Cool in pans on rack for 10 minutes. Remove from pans; let cool completely on rack. Place 1 layer on a serving plate and spread with dulce de leche. Top with banana slices. Top with second layer of cake.

4 Combine chocolate and cream in a small saucepan on medium-low heat. Cook and stir continuously until chocolate is almost melted. Remove from heat. Stir until chocolate is completely melted. Cool until slightly thick. Spoon chocolate over cake, allowing it to run down the sides. Before chocolate sets, sprinkle with nuts, if you'd like. Serve immediately.

Makes 12 to 14 servings.

Serve this cake as soon as you make it so the bananas don't turn brown.

Count with Boots! How many banana slices do you see?

FAMILY FIESTA

SEE MENUS WITH MAP, PAGE 122

Howling Wolf Bars

DAY AT THE BEACH
SEE MENUS WITH MAP, PAGE 122

ingredients

- 1   cup flaked coconut
-      Nonstick cooking spray
- 2   cups rolled oats
- 1½   cups white whole wheat flour
- 1   teaspoon baking powder
- ½   teaspoon salt
- 2   eggs, lightly beaten
- ½   cup granulated sugar
- ½   cup packed brown sugar
- 2   tablespoons canola oil
- 1   teaspoon vanilla extract
- 1   apple, peeled, cored, and chopped (about ¾ cup)
- 1½   cups semisweet chocolate pieces

The toasted coconut topping on these bars looks a little bit like the fur on a wolf. Take a bite and then howl like a wolf!

Let's make it! ¡A la aventura!

1 Preheat oven to 350°F. Spread coconut in a single layer in a shallow baking pan. Bake for 5 to 10 minutes or until lightly golden brown, stirring occasionally. Cool and set aside.

2 Coat a 13x9-inch baking pan with nonstick cooking spray. In a medium bowl, combine oats, flour, baking powder, and salt. In a large bowl, combine eggs, sugars, oil, and vanilla. Add flour mixture and apple to egg mixture and stir until combined. With a clean damp hand, press evenly into prepared pan.

3 Bake for 20 to 25 minutes until toothpick inserted in center comes out clean. Remove from oven and sprinkle with chocolate pieces. Return to oven for 1 to 2 minutes until chocolate is softened. Spread chocolate evenly over surface. Immediately sprinkle with toasted coconut. When completely cooled, cut into 25 bars.

Makes 25 bars.

Baby Sea Turtle Cupcakes

ingredients

1¼ cups white whole wheat flour

1 teaspoon baking powder

¼ teaspoon baking soda

¼ teaspoon salt

⅔ cup granulated sugar

¼ cup butter (½ stick), at room temperature

½ teaspoon vanilla extract

1 egg

¾ cup low-fat plain yogurt

1¼ cups purchased or homemade vanilla frosting

blue and green food coloring

gum drops

candy-coated chocolate candies

Let's make it! *¡A la aventura!*

1 Preheat oven to 350°F. Line 12 muffin cups with paper liners.

2 In a medium bowl, combine flour, baking powder, baking soda, and salt; set aside.

3 In a large mixing bowl, beat together sugar, butter, and vanilla on medium for 1 to 2 minutes until well combined. Add egg and beat for 1 minute.

4 Add the flour mixture, alternating with yogurt, in 3 portions, beating after each addition. Scrape down sides of bowl with rubber spatula as needed.

5 Divide batter among muffin cups. Bake for 15 to 20 minutes or until a toothpick inserted into centers comes out clean. Cool completely on rack.

6 In a small bowl, tint frosting with a little blue and green food coloring to make the color aqua. Frost cupcakes and decorate with candies to look like turtles.

Makes 12 cupcakes.

Note: If you'd like, use your favorite boxed cake mix. Decorate 12 cupcakes and save the remaining 12 for another use.

La Princesa Dora's Castle

ingredients

- 2 2-layer boxed cake mixes
- 6 cups purchased or favorite homemade vanilla frosting
- Purple icing tint
- 4 sugar cones
- graham crackers
- assorted candies
- decorating sugars and candies
- ribbon flags

Let's make it! ¡Vámonos!

1. In a large bowl, prepare 2 cake mixes at once according to package directions. Line four 2½-inch muffin cups with paper liners. Prepare 3 round 9-inch pans according to package directions. Fill muffin cups two-thirds full; divide remaining batter among 9-inch pans and bake according to package directions.

2. If you'd like, cut top off of 9-inch cakes to create a flat surface. Cut tops from cupcakes to make flat surfaces and remove papers. Set aside ¼ cup vanilla frosting. Tint remaining frosting purple.

3. Place one 9-inch cake in center of cake plate. Frost top; arrange second cake on top and frost top. Arrange remaining cake on top; frost top and sides.

4. Arrange 4 cupcakes top sides down around cake edge. Frost cupcakes.

5. Melt reserved frosting for 30 seconds to 1 minute in microwave. Brush on outside of 1 cone and immediately sprinkle with decorative sugar or sprinkles. Set aside to dry. Repeat with other cones. Place on cupcakes, point sides up. Insert ribbon flags into cones.

6. Using graham crackers, candies, and sugars decorate cake to look like a castle.

Makes 16 servings.

¡Feliz cumpleaños!
Happy birthday!
You can help
decorate the castle
for one royal
party!

DORA'S BIRTHDAY PARTY
SEE MENUS WITH MAP, PAGE 122

121

MENUS WITH Map!

A meal is made up of different foods that taste good together. That's called a menu. Map can help you make menus with the recipes in this book. Can you find these symbols on the recipe pages to make great menus?

Day at the Beach

SNACK #1 Find the food that you dip in dressing!

_____

SNACK #2 Find the recipe that has pretzels in it!

_____

SNACK #3 Find the food that has coconut on top!

_____

Tapas Party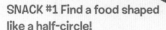

SNACK #1 Find a food shaped like a half-circle!

_____

SNACK #2 Find a food that is small and round!

_____

SNACK #3 Find a recipe that uses peanut butter!

_____

SNACK #4 Find the recipe with pineapple in it!

_____

Dora's Birthday Party

DRINK Find a recipe that has two kinds of fruit juice!

_____

MAIN DISH Find a food that has a crunchy coating!

_____

SIDE DISH Find a recipe that mixes fruit and veggies!

_____

DESSERT Find a food fit for royalty!

_____

Rise and Shine

DRINK Find a two-color drink!

_____

MAIN DISH Find food shaped like a bird's home!

_____

BREAD Find a recipe with fruit that is small, round, and blue!

_____

Farmers' Market Feast

MAIN DISH Find a recipe that has spinach in it for one of the choices!

_____

SIDE DISH Find a food that will make you laugh!

_____

DESSERT Find a dessert that lets you dip!

_____

Family Fiesta

MAIN DISH Find a recipe with snow peas in it!

_____

DRINK Find a recipe with rice in it!

_____

DESSERT Find food with bananas in the middle!

_____

Diego's Rainforest Fiesta

SNACK Find a food shaped like an animal!

_____

MAIN DISH Find a food that has "trees" in it!

_____

SIDE DISH Find a food you get to build yourself!

_____

DESSERT Find a food that looks like a sea creature!

_____

Cooking with Abuela

SOUP Find a recipe with corn in it!

_____

MAIN DISH Find a dish you get to pile up high!

_____

DESSERT Find a recipe that has oats in it!

_____

Whole Wheat Refrigerator Dough

ingredients

- 2 packages active dry yeast
- 2 cups warm water (110°F to 115°F)
- ½ cup sugar
- 2 teaspoons salt
- 4½ cups unbleached all-purpose flour
- 1 egg
- ¼ cup canola oil
- 2 cups whole wheat flour

Let's make it! ¡Vámonos!

1 In a large mixing bowl, dissolve yeast in water. Let stand 5 minutes or until yeast is dissolved.

2 Add sugar, salt, and 3 cups of the all-purpose flour. Beat with an electric mixer on low speed until moistened. Beat 2 minutes at medium speed. Beat in egg and oil.

3 Using a wooden spoon, stir in whole wheat flour and enough of the remaining all-purpose flour to make a soft dough.

4 Turn out onto a lightly floured surface. Knead until dough is smooth and elastic, about 6 to 8 minutes. Place in a greased bowl, turning once to grease top. Cover with plastic wrap and let rise until doubled or cover and refrigerate overnight.

5 Punch dough down and form into desired shapes. Place on a greased baking pan. Cover and let rise at room temperature until doubled, about 1 hour for dough prepared the same day or 1 to 2 hours for refrigerated dough. For Silly Snake Sticks (page 36), let rise only 10 to 15 minutes.

6 Bake in a 375°F oven for 10 to 12 minutes or until golden brown.

Note: Dough may be kept up to 4 days in the refrigerator. Punch down daily.

Simple Whole Wheat Pastry Dough

ingredients

- 2 cups unbleached all-purpose flour
- ⅔ cup whole wheat flour
- ½ teaspoon salt
- ½ cup canola oil
- 6 to 8 tablespoons low-fat milk

Let's make it! ¡Vámonos!

1 In a large mixing bowl, stir together all-purpose flour, whole wheat flour, and salt. Add oil and 6 tablespoons milk all at once to flour mixture. Stir lightly with a fork until combined. If necessary, stir in 1 to 2 tablespoons additional milk to moisten (pastry will look crumbly.) Form pastry into a ball.

2 Divide dough in half. Form each half into a ball. On a lightly floured surface, slightly flatten 1 pastry ball. Using a rolling pin, roll dough from center to edges into a circle about 13 inches in diameter (press any cracks that appear together). Use to make empanadas (page 40). Or, ease pastry circle into a 9-inch pie plate without stretching it. Trim pastry to ½ inch beyond edge of pie plate. Fill and bake pastry as directed in individual recipe for single- or double-crust pie. Makes 2 piecrusts (8 servings for a double-crust pie; 16 servings for 2 single-crust pies).

Bake Pastry Shell: For a single baked shell, prepare as above, but prick the bottom and sides of the pastry with a fork. Line pastry with a double thickness of foil. Bake in a 450°F oven for 8 minutes. Remove foil. Bake 5 to 6 minutes more until crust is golden. Cool on a wire rack.

Note: If your recipe calls for a single crust, you can freeze the remaining dough. Flatten it slightly into a disk, then wrap tightly in plastic wrap and store in a sealed plastic bag in the freezer for up to 3 months. Unwrap to thaw so condensation doesn't make the dough soggy.

Fruits and Veggies Log

Eating lots of fruits and vegetables makes you healthy and strong. Be a fruit-and-vegetable explorer and try something new! Keep track of the fruits and vegetables you eat every day of the week in this log. Looking at it will make you so proud!

Day of the Week	Fruits and Veggies Eaten	Number of Fruits	Number of Veggies
Sunday			
Monday			
Tuesday			
Wednesday			
Thursday			
Friday			
Saturday			

Can you count las frutas y los vegetales you ate today?

125

INDEX